# Understanding Behaviour
## An overview to your best friends behaviour
### by Lisa Hansen

The challenge of dog behaviour is something that we all can use a little help with. This book is an overview of some of the things we should consider as dog owners, trainers or shelter workers. There is no simple answers to behaviour, behaviour is a complex mix of past present and genetics. This is not only about the dog but it is about us as trainer, handlers and coaches to others who own dogs.
No two dogs are alike and no two owners trainers or handlers are alike either, it's time to celebrate and understand the differences, it is not time to conform. Building our skills comes through understanding behaviour and recognising our dogs strengths and weaknesses. If we can truely train the dog in front of us then we are bound to have a long and happy partnership with our pet.

**A brief history of the dog human partnership**

When considering any work with the canine family it's important to understand where they came from and how they became the companion they are today. What is it that defines the species? The term Canidae is the family name given to all modern dogs, there are 35 species within this family group including the wolf and coyote. The species canidae are omnivores who eat a wide range of food including scavenging. The domestic dog as we know it today has a set of genomes that were inherited from wolves, but not wolves as we know them today, they and the modern wolf also somewhere in the dark and distant past through a process of evolution have also changed from the ancient line of wolves so that todays domesticated dog and the modern wolf are both as removed from the original wolf genomes as each other.
The story about how they separated out from the original wolf DNA and became what they are today is still under debate, was there one domestication event or was there two separate areas of domestication? Was the first dog a wolf pup taken home by hunters and made into a family pet, or where the first domesticated dogs simply opportunists that found it easier to live close to humans and share their food sources. Whatever the event that bought about the domestic dog what

we do know through the Belyven fox project is that it is only a matter of generations for a wild animal to become domesticated, and once the process begins other significant changes in the animal's characteristics take place as well. In this instance foxes were chosen by their flight distance, flight distance being the distance in which the animal takes flight, did the fox run to the back of the cage basically or stay close to the front. This was the criteria for the to become a part of the breeding program and within a short period of time the flight distance decreased even more and canine like behaviours began to be exhibited by the off spring of the original subjects, these subjects then began as they became friendlier and more dog like to change other fox characteristic, their pointy ears became floppy, their coat colours began to change. Behaviour went from not being stand offish to be dog like friendly whimpering and calling for attention from human handlers. Today black and white foxes are bred as pets. In this instance, a process of artificial selection was made with limited parameters', these parameters were changed after the foxes began to change so dramatically that the original criteria became more common and the selection process was redefined. The foxes were then selected on more canine like behaviours in response to the huge changes in the foxes behaviour.

So we can assume from this that flight distance has a huge part to play in the domestication of any animal. If we break up the instinctual response of the dog to the fight or flight response and we think about how that impacts on the response of the dog then we begin to see how the wolf would respond to human interactions. Then we put the circle out 5 meters ten meters 30 meters and it becomes obvious that the wolf who does not take flight until 5 meters may be more susceptible to human contact. Evolution would see the wolves with the most relaxed flight distance be less fearful of humans and allow for them to observe and watch and wait for humans to be useful to them. When it was obvious that humans were useful perhaps as a food source wolves lost some of their defensive behaviours and started to become the domestic dog of today. We know from the Belyven fox project that the ears changing shape were one of the first points of change in the foxes as their flight distance continued to diminish.

Natural selection could also play a part in the separation of domestic dog from wolves, Natural selection suggests that the characteristics most suited to survival will be those carried genetically through the pack, for the modern wolf there is little variation due to the needs of the pack and the individual animals, they need keen hearing, good eyesight, and strong bodies to hunt, Natural selection would also decree that the flight distance would also remain further/wider and the wolves therefore continue down a narrower epigenetic pathway, the domestic dog however found benefits in the protection and friendship of human and through a process of artificial selection and relaxed selection the dogs became many and varied as we see today.

Theories of Domestication

There are four real theories of domestication, none are proved as such: Theory 1 the wolf cub, a cub was stolen from the pack or found and picked up and taken home, the advantages of the wolf as it grew, alerting to strangers, helping with the hunt, keeping vermin away from stored food, became apparent and so started the domestic dog. Co-evolution is another theory as already discussed man and Wolf found a mutual benefit in sharing the pathway. Cultural Evolution the principal that humans found wolves to be of benefit to them and refined the dog as they went along. Finally, Population selection- dogs finding their way to humans perhaps via the rubbish dump and found them useful for scavenging food, this reduced their flight distance and may even have given wolves who may not have survived in a natural environment a chance to thrive and even breed.

Epigenetic Influence

Epigenetic influence plays a big role in the ongoing changes to the wolves, while it does not affect the DNA of the wolf it is impacted by the environment, if the weather is cold the coat grows thicker and faster, if the prey is big the dogs will be bigger and faster to catch it, they may even have a different set of skills that will become evident in the hunt to ensure their survival. The flopping ears and coat changes are an epigenetic influence that begins the domestication process. The wild wolf needs grey coat to blend in more easily with its environment and in the wild a red and white wolf may not survive due to lack of camouflage but in a domestic environment that same wolf has reduced risk and easier meals has less need to blend in to ensure its belly is full, they may even be more appealing to human and there for better fed, coat or other epigenetic influence then become more prevalent in the following generations as the environmental changes become more stable.

Domestication

Here starts the journey of domestication. It is always to be remembered that the dog as we know it has become domesticated, has evolved and changed to become the faithful companion that they are today. But they maintain the DNA influence of the ancient Wolf.

How dogs learn and how they have become the dog they are today, has its starting place in genetics and epigenetic influence but dogs like humans learn through a series of different techniques, some positive some not so positive. To get the most out of any style training though we need to understand the learning process types of intelligence. Having an understanding of the learning theory helps us to be better trainers and to get better happier results. When we look at learning theory and what that means we understand that there are many factors that play a part in learning, cognitive thinking, emotional and environmental influences and past experiences. While we look at the way that animals and specifically the way dogs learn I think it is important for us to remember that these factors apply to our own individual learning as well, and our past experiences and emotional feelings have an important part to play in the way that we learn and teach. To believe that dog training was just about the dog would be a mistake on the part of the handler, a bad day for either the dog or their handler may well make or break the regime, undermine confidence or even offer consequence that bring about the wrong type of learning.

Nature versus nurture

Nature verses nurture is also a big player in the learning debate, Is every dog perfect? Is every dog capable of happy ever after? If this is the case then every handler must be capable of training each dog  in an appropriate way to bring about positive and lasting change. The theory that temperament is set totally by nature is relevant, inherited genetic code and ancestral history certainly have a place in determining the outcome of any animal's behaviour, Nature suggests that these are the only things that matter, Nurture on the other hand suggests that any dog any time anywhere would be perfect should they have the right care and does not allow for genetic inheritance that predetermines outcomes. That their ability to learn from their environment over rides their nature. Is there such a thing as a bad dog the answer is vague and not for the faint hearted. Sadly, nature plays a role in all individuals human and Canine alike, and just as humans have emotional and mental health issues so to can our canine friends. Just as some cultures have idiosyncrasies that are specific to their race so do some breeds of dogs, add to this, their breed dispositions their environmental and emotional circumstances, throw in a bit of past history and a dog can well be a ticking time bomb waiting for a trigger to respond. Breed disposition can play a huge role in the temperaments of any individuals so it is important take this into consideration when training or working with individual animals. For my own experience I work almost entirely with rescue dogs, and their handlers, In shelter you can see straight away breed characteristics and you can pick the responses that you know will take place in any given set of circumstances, you know that English staffy crosses will have separation anxiety and be human focused, you know that American staffys will tend towards aggression towards other dogs in the shelter, and fence fighting, that they are big and strong and capable and they know it, you know that Chihuahuas will make every one believe that they are cold even when it is 40 degrees, (we live in the tropics) does this mean that each of the dogs labeled will be exactly the same with the same outcomes, of course not, but what it does mean is that right from day one you can observe the animal and see the behaviour and you know what behaviour modification plans   will need to be put into place to reduce trigger stacking and to bring about a scenario that sees the dog safely in its forever home as quickly as possible.

It is also possible to manage the behaviours from day one, reduce stress, limit barking behaviour use of essential oils or other techniques to reduce the building of stress, exercise and training support positive outcomes. You also know that when it goes bad that you have to be firm and strong in managing poor behaviours to ensure no one human or animal is hurt.

For our shelter our dogs are generally a staffy(Bully) cross breed, big and bred indiscriminately. We see signs up on the notice board, Puppies for sale, great hunters, guard dogs or children's pets.  Which is it? Because these characteristics do not always sit well in the same dog. Are the dogs bred to work and fight and chase, to guard, or are they bred to be lap dogs. The lack of clear and precise bloodlines and the throwing in of any breed that may make the dog faster more resilient or more aggressive. This mish mash of genetics causes breed confusion and what we are finding is that we have these huge dogs with limited manners and sometimes no positive dog experience, some perhaps even suffering from social depravation then dumped at the pound or just left in rental properties

The tragedy compounds with handlers taking home a cute puppy, plays with, loves, for the early days and then as the puppy who is finally vaccinated is ready for walking finding the dog is so huge and so bouncy and the handers are out of control from day one. Spoilt puppy, no manners, tiny handler's, giant dogs. Behaviour modification for handlers as well as the dog is essential. The dog so big, pulls so hard, the owners are scared to walk them the dog gets left in the yard and misses critical social interaction. Social depravation turns into something resembling aggression and our dog is reactive with a handler who does not know how to respond well, the dog sits in the back yard and the cycle spins on. The handler gets a transfer dog is not valued and dog is then left behind. Experience plays a big role in the learning theory and brings about success for our organisation. Every dog goes home with behaviour lessons or puppy school to encourage experience and positive handling.

Ethology

The science of ethology observes animals in their natural state, for dogs that natural state is now amidst humans.

Ethology is the scientific and objective study of animals, the focus of ethology to study to be done under natural conditions. The study of ethology sees behaviour as an evolutionary and adaptive trait. Ethology is focused on behaviour, and looks at the epigenetic influence on behaviour through evolution.

It is important that we observe behaviours in the natural, in an environment where the dog is not stressed. What is their natural behaviour, can we even see this in a shelter situation. How does this impact on their stress levels? How much does breed play a role, (epigenetic influence) How much does environment play a role. When we look at natural behaviour we are no longer looking back to the wolf and determining behaviour patterns from the modern-day wolf, instead we are looking at the development of the dog in human partnership. Finding out what is the natural behaviour is an important key to any future behaviour management. Doing this in a shelter environment is very difficult and makes foster carers and their observations hugely important to finding a natural and non-stressed (hopefully) behaviour. If we are unable to physically view an animal's environment then listening to the handler and their concerns and finding out the full history is of equal value to our training plans. The observation of the human behaviour linked to the dog is also essential in any behaviour planning. It is no point setting a plan that is beyond the scope of the handler. In the case of fostering of animals it is important to match the dog carefully to the carer so that we give both the best chance of success.

One of the things we do as trainers is to see dogs in stressed environments, in group settings so we need to be sure that our training methods are relative to the environment we are in. To work with a shelter dog in a shelter environment we need to consider the trigger stacks and to ensure we are enabling enough positive input to put the dog at ease, the dog is not going to learn when he is in a position of fight or flight, when his body is shut down into stress and his brain has switched off. It is important to bring about positive and calm changes to the dog and its environment to ensure that he can learn. Dopamine is an important tool for learning in any environment and it is significantly increased by positive interactions. Humans too learn well from encouragement. The positives trigger the neurotransmitters and bring about positive and longer lasting changes, this process though needs to happen over longer periods of time four or five weeks even, be built layer upon layer to achieve a new learning pathway. Owners/handlers need to be watched for the right consequences for behaviours and the dogs themselves need to be closely observed for responses to behaviour. Missing key positives can reduce the success of behaviour modification.

Types of training

For some people training dogs is a bit intuitive and for many individuals they think they know about animals and dogs in particular, for some this is a lucky happen stance and they do ok with their dogs. It is only when they encounter a dog outside of the normal behaviour traits that they discover they really do not know anything about behaviours. Understanding the theory of learning gives a trainer or handler a better understanding of how dogs learn, the opportunities for different styles and methods of training, and also helps to understand the way an individual animal learns. An understanding of the learning theory gives us opportunity to be able to deliver training to our dogs that is specific to their learning capabilities. Understanding the learning theory gives us opportunity to offer positive communication with our dog for maximum effect, and minimal effort. Growing the skill set involved in training giving the handler confidence will increase the effectiveness of any training. It will also increase the bond between dog and handler lessening the risk of abandonment at a later date.

There are four quadrants of learning and BF Skinner tested all the quadrants of learning through his experiments. His study helps us to better understand types of learning and gives us an opportunity to teach better, If we apply the techniques to human learning and apply what we know to the Team – Handler and Dog rather than just the individual it will increase our opportunities for success.

The four learning quadrants are:

<u>Positive reinforcement</u>- adding something that the dog likes to encourage a given behaviour. Adding treats to the training regime so that the dog will offer positive behaviours to receive treats

<u>Negative reinforcement</u>- removing a negative so the dog believes that his behaviour stopped the pain, a dog in a prong collar stops pulling collar stops causing pain, dog believes that walking nicely prevents pain.

<u>Positive punishment</u>- adding something ie an electric shock to a behaviour so that the recipient believes their negative behaviour caused the pain

<u>Negative punishment</u>- removing something the dog likes ie a toy when the dog is behaving poorly so that the dog believes his poor behaviour caused the loss of the toy. We sometimes use this in teaching a dog to stay on a mat, if the dog stands up the handler steps back, when the dog sits down the handler steps closer to the dog. The reward being the handler coming closer to the Dog. So taking the learning theory we can then apply the methods of training, operant conditioning, classical conditioning, counter conditioning. Understanding these allows us to make

an educated decision on the best method for the circumstances and the expected outcomes for these methods. I.e. if we chose to use a method that requires positive punishment and the method involved a pinch collar we would have an expectation that the dog would associate poor behaviour with pain and in the absence of the pinch collar may not perform the positive behaviours that have been targeted by the use of the pinch collar. Equally an all positive rewards base method without consequence may not offer the best solution if rewards are food based and not available at all times.

Operant conditioning is a conscious effort to change a behaviour, as with Skinners experiments with the rats in the box he conditioned the rats to understand that the light meant a shock and if they pushed the lever then the bad thing wouldn't happen. The premise is that the animal learns through consequences. The consequence of not learning means that the rat will be shocked. The conditioning takes place over a period of time and is depended on the capacity of the animal to learn. This is a method that trains: "behaviour equals outcome", good or bad the theory is by offering a particular outcome to any given behaviour will result in a training of the behaviour. So, if a poor behaviour is rewarded by a positive behaviour then the animal will likely learn from the reward and continue with the poor behaviour. Reinforcement of behaviour suggests that any reinforcement of positive behaviour will result in continuing of the positive behaviour.

Punishment as a form of behaviour modification is of limited use without positive reinforcement and training of positive behaviours.

It is unrealistic to think that a dog can only be trained on negatives just like humans they need the positive input to increase their learning capacity and to grow neural pathways.  Punishment as a form of training only increases the dogs fear responses and can encourage the dog towards learned helplessness rather than true learning. Punishment reduces the dog's ability to learn and the brains ability to develop the neural pathways that lead to learning development.

Classical conditioning as per Pavlov's dog supports the theory that a given stimuli will give a specific response. Classical conditioning associates two things in the participants mind, in the case of Pavlov's dog it was food and a bell. The dog who was excited and salivated over his food, then transferred that excitement to the bell. The bell rang the dog would salivate in anticipation.  We use classical conditioning with the clicker, the click means a reward is coming, Counter conditioning on the other hand is the process of changing a particular behaviour, the methodology is that the by adding a low-level fear trigger and exposing the subject to a positive experience while the negative is low key in the back ground that the subject can be re-conditioned to see the fear trigger as less threatening. Hopefully even bringing the behaviour to extinction.

Counter conditioning is a form of training that could be used were the stimuli was something like storm phobia, where possibly a taped storm is playing lightly in the back ground while exposing the dog to positive experiences shaping a more positive response to the underlying fear trigger.


Physical health

Physical health is important when looking at canine behaviour because like human's canines can be adversely affected through lack of nutrition and issues with immune systems, a dog that lives constantly in fight or flight has a system deprived of full growth and nutrient required for development and for brain growth. For ourselves if we are not eating a balanced diet or sleeping well or have underlying health issues it can make our behaviour less positive when dealing with others, stress impacts hugely on our responses to others and for the dog it is no different. Without adequate nutrition as opposed to adequate food then the dog has no ability to regulate its emotions or responses. Having a holistic approach to health and behaviour ensures that our dogs are better able to deal with daily stress and the activities that life holds. The Autonomic
Nervous System is the part of the nervous system that deals with stress. It is the part of the body that deals with unconscious actions. The stress trigger causes the body to release cortisol and adrenaline to help the body immobilize for danger. While the body is in a state of stress all other non-essential systems function at a reduced capacity, just as in some people are unable to eat when their bodies are stressed so too does living in stress environment effect the dogs ability to digest its food and for the body to maintain immune system and other bodily functions that help to maintain healthy attitude and happy disposition. Cortisol is released into the body as a response to fear or stress, it is a key part of the flight or fight mechanism that is released by the adrenal glands. Its role is to divert energy into the body to increase muscle strength and reactivity of the body. Increasing breathing capabilities, all the things required by the dog to make its fight or flight successful and to increase strength in the animal. During this process though these energy or nutrients are diverted from other areas of the body such as the immune system the learning part of the brain and other key functions. A dog under long term stress can then have other issues which are associated to stress. i.e. lowered immunity, poor skin and poor growth rates.

 I feel that often we under estimate the benefit of good food and a diet that is well considered to match the needs of the dog concerned. Humans who have poor diets have issues with sleep, headaches and other irritabilities that effect not only their body but their behaviour as well. As an anxiety sufferer I know that anxiety causes gut reactions and other responses that reduce my ability to focus and to even some times be productive, if we apply the things we know about human stress to our canine companions who have after all evolve to live in harmony with us then we have to assume that some of our traits have been genetically enhanced by a process of artificial selection. Anxious and reactive dogs in a pre-evolutionary life would have found assimilation into the working life of the pack difficult but with artificial selection these traits make the dogs attractive to their human companions. The long term symptoms of stress can include Depression, loss of sleep, stomach ulcers, Hypertension and slowed growth, overall long term stress can cause significant issues with the bodies whole body being in distress because of the long term stress, while we tend to think of the stress triggers being external i.e. loud noises, poor living environments, the stress can be triggered by over vaccination, poor quality food and other such impacts which can also reduce the immunity system and in its turn the rest of the bodies organs including the skin and digestive symptoms. keeps the dog on high alert

Neurons are the nerve cells and nerve fibers that make up the brain, each individual cell is a complicated design which needs to be fully functioning for signals to be passed through the brain, without the neurons the brain ceases to function. These cells interlock and quickly pass information from one cell to the next. Damaged or degraded cells reduce the brains efficiency and ability to transmit information

Without a healthy body and without a healthy digestive system the process of osmosis fails to supply nutrients to the body this reduces all the bodies functions including the ability of neurons to re-generate and to continue to transmit much needed information through the body.

The neurotransmitter Noradrenaline is the neurotransmitter that triggers the body into action during stress occurrences, it redirects critical energy to parts of the body required to function in flight or fight capacity. For example, the muscles ready to run. The reverse side of this is that it raises the heart rate, reduces the flow of blood to the gastrointestinal system and keeps the dog on high alert

Digestion is important to the dog health without the digestive system in complete working order the dogs body cannot process the nutrients, without nutrients the dogs body is not able to fully function, poor nutrition, inability to digest, all lead to unhealthy dog, the immune system relies on the nutrients provided through the digestive system to supply the immunity cells with the resources they need to kill harmful cells, to grow skin and hair to maintain energy. The digestive system is responsible for the health of every cell in the body. It is important for us to ensure that our dogs digestive system is as healthy as possible, we do this through good quality food that has the nutrients that our dogs need. A Healthy digestive system allows for processing of food once chewed, passing it through the gastric system to break down the nutrients that can be gathered from food, then dispersing the food throughout the body, through a process of osmosis. Waste elimination is also an important part of this digestive system and includes elimination through the kidneys and liver, bowels and skin. Without elimination of the waste toxins build up in the body causing poor health complications and organ failure. To ensure good digestion we need to ensure that the nervous system is also fully function, the role that stress plays cannot be discounted.

Always remembering that any sudden onset of behaviour change should be checked with a Vet, there are often things that can be picked up that we as owners or even trainers have never considered, sudden onset aggression particularly needs checking to ensure that there is nothing that prevents the dog from learning and growing, and to ensure that there is no ongoing health related problems. Ruling out health enables us to focus on the triggers and helps to resolve behaviour issues.
It is not legal or ethical for a non-Veterinarian to diagnose health in an animal. It is therefore important that should a Behaviour Professional or owner suspect that behaviour issues stem from health issues then the animal is referred to a Veterinarian. As a Behaviour Professional though it is important that we understand the impacts that health can have on behaviour so that owners can be given sound support in their endeavors to support their pets.


Behaviour

Any behaviour plan has to take into account all aspects of the dog's life, but it also needs to take into account the handler, what the handler wants to achieve and what the handler is willing to contribute to the plan. Observation is key to ensuring that we can determine the style and the type of approach that both handler and dog require. There is no point training the handler in treat based methodology if the dog doesn't enjoy food and is not food motivated. Observation is also key to ensuring that we understand the communication style between dog and handler and if it is working, using the ABC method we can ensure that we are understanding the consequences of the behaviours both the dogs and the Handlers. We may well ask what does the term ABC mean?
The term ABC means Antecedent – What happens before a behaviour, the thing that could be the trigger, the trigger it has to be remembered is not always seen, the trigger can be an allergy, a past bad experience that was handled poorly, poor digestive system, there are many factors that can precede a behaviour. Trigger

stacking is when a stressor is present for a dog the trigger could be strangers walking past, loud noises, too much chemical residue in the body, basically the dog is in a constant state of stress and the recovery time between one trigger and the next become reduce and non- existent and the dog than becomes reactive and unable to resolve the stressors. Because the dog's neurotransmitters are releasing chemicals into the body that prepared the dog for fight or flight the dog then lives in a state of constant arousal the dog cannot reason through the stressors, the brain is triggered by the hindbrain and the for-brain is not functioning. To reduce the trigger stacking the dog needs to be completely removed from the triggers and given the opportunity for its body functions to return to normal, so that its systems and thinking capabilities are restored.

 Dopamine is the feel-good neurotransmitter; this chemical is released by the neurons to send signals to other parts of the body. Dopamine is useful in motivating behaviour, strengthening memory and even regulating body movements. Lack of dopamine can lead to depression amongst other symptoms.
Dopamine Is released into the body when using rewards based training, dopamine encourages learning and development of neural pathways, as ethical trainers it is important to teach our clients how to use positive methods to train their dogs.

Serotonin is also considered a happy neurotransmitter it is said to regulate anxiety reduce depression assist in healing wounds encourages bone health, it's often found in the stomach and it is basically the natural mood stabilizer produced by the body. Promoting healthy sleeping pattern helping with digestion,

B is for Behaviour- Behaviour is an outward expression of inward emotion. The outwards behaviour gives significant information about the inner health of a dog and allows us to create a plan to help to modify behaviours that are perhaps not family healthy behaviours.

So then what is the behaviour? How does it look? a behaviour is anything good or bad that may or may not affect the relationship with the handler or others in the dogs environment, and it is important to understand what is a natural behaviour that can be expected and should be managed and what is a learned behaviour that can be retrained with proper planning. Natural behaviours such as digging or cocking its leg are not behaviours that we would be considering problem behaviours. In the same way a dog that sits and looks sad eyed everytime you go to the fridge is also a learned behaviour, not good or bad just a behaviour chances are the behaviour are rewarded every time it is repeated so no matter if the reward is from the handler or whether the dog is self-rewarding this leads to consequence.

C is for Consequence- this is what happened after the behaviour took place, the dog dug a hole, got a lot of attention from the handler because it was digger, or alternatively found a nice cool/warm spot to lay in, enjoyed the scents of fresh earth ate worms, whatever the reward for the behaviour is and found themselves well rewarded for the behaviour. The dog looking sad eyed sitting by the fridge has learnt this is a behaviour that is rewarded, even if it isn't rewarded every time with food the verbalisation or other communication from the handler is likely to be positive and encouraging and the dog knows that if he continues to perform the behaviour eventually he will get the reward. The best way to ensure that a reward sticks is through random re-enforcement so one or two pats or accidental food drops is enough to encourage the behaviour into perpetuity. Consequences can maintain a behaviour through the following: -escaping something when the behaviour is shown-  dog cringes when handler says no, handler doesn't follow through,  - dog gets a reward from the behaviour- dog jumps on hander when he sees them handler pats dog, dog is rewarded for the behaviour, Something is providing a functional reward by the behaviour- dog has food handler moves to take food dog growls handler backs away, dog wins. d) something is avoided via the behaviour- handler wants to go home dog won't be caught, dog avoids going home and gets extra play time

You can use an ABC chart any time you are working with a client and their dog, in fact you could use the ABC chart any time you are working with any dog for any behaviour. Although the Antecedent-past may not be visible or known especially for example in a rescue dog it is still an important tool for working with any dog and any behaviour. In the situation where you are monitoring and working with shelter dogs you can use this as part of the behaviour modification plan, the observation is going to be different in a high stress situation but is still relevant to the individual and the handler. In fact observation becomes more critical and more useful as the dog has multiple handlers.

Kindness matters

Everything that we do with dogs needs to be done in a manner that is holistic and covers all aspects of the animal's life and capabilities. No one cure will work on every animal and it is incredibly important for us to be able to observe and see what is really happening in any given situation, and while especially in a shelter situation we can view the animal by comparison with other dogs who have come through a similar experience, it is the history or antecedent that is unseen that can contribute to the ongoing behaviour and stress levels of any dog. A dog that has lived in social isolation is not going to find the kennels a stress free environment. A dog that has been in the pound next to another dog who is fence fighting, or water aggressive or constantly barking is going to have a stack of triggers waiting to explode with any new triggers that come along. Step one in any behaviour management plan therefor needs to be an understanding of all that goes before. It has to take into consideration evolution DNA breed disposition learning theory observation health stress nervous system this is the starting point.

Step one observation

a. What do you see?

b. How does the dog look ?

c. Is the dog stressed or relaxed?

d. Does the dog know you are there?

e. Do we see the dog focused and responding or do we see a dog in fight or flight mode.

f. Is the dog healthy?

It is important to learn to see beyond the painted picture to understand what we are looking at, the act of observing is incredibly important. Understanding what we are observing is even more important.

Step two of the behaviour modification is environment.

Can we change the environment? If we can what is the response of the dog to the new environment? Does it add an extra stress trigger to the dog? Alternatively does it allow the dog to relax and calm and begin to release the stress? How do we do this? We start with a functional assessment we ask a series of questions, Questions to be asked

a. What is your greatest concern behaviourally- What do those behaviours look like?

b. What is the respondent behaviour? The behaviour that happens immediately after a trigger ie a balloon popping?

c.  What is the recovery like?

d.  Does the dog have any know health issues?

e.  Is there any one thing that triggers the behaviour in the dog?

f.  How much exercise or work is the dog getting?

g.  What is the experience/skill level of the handler?

h.  Has something happened recently to bring about changes in the behaviour?

There are three main reasons for behaviours to change
psychological changes- the dog may have a constantly high stress level and this may cause behaviour changes from less tolerant to sleeping all day to aggression.

Medical changes- the dog may be subject to medication that has side effects that could cause behaviour changes from aggression through to in-appetent to lethargic

Biological changes – the biological nature of the dog should never be overlooked breed considerations should be taken in to consideration if a dog behaviours changes perhaps the biological aspect of the dog's nature is not being considered

All these things are equally as important to our observation but the questions are based on the person and the things affecting the dog. In this instance, we are focusing our plan on the behaviour management of shelter animals so we need to determine what environmental factors are impacting on the dog, we get a short window of opportunity to observe and get the plan right, the dogs will need to go into a foster situation and we want their environment to be one that is conducive to the long-term well-being of the dog. There is a short window of opportunity to test the behaviour, determine the plan and give the dog to the right foster parent. Without proper choosing the dog returns and then we begin to add other concerns to the animal's welfare and well-being and we add stress triggers to the dog. Each of these things are concerning in themselves because they put the dog in a position that reduces their re-home ability. If we truly want to reduce euthanasia rates and to ensure more adoptions then this is a critical time in the dogs life. This is the time when the plan needs to be right. For dogs who are easy in behaviour and easy to home the plan is insignificant, but for those who are teetering on behaviour, stress impact can quickly produce a reactive dog that is difficult to place.

Respondant behaviour is the instant and natural behaviour that happens should a trigger appear i.e. a firework exploding the dog starts it's a natural response. How does this affect future behaviours, future behaviour is affected by the consequence, the dog starts at the fireworks gets a lot of attention for his start, it pays dividends the dog finds it worth his while to start at noises and display behaviour that gets attention and pats or praise.

That consequence can maintain in a behaviour we would rather not be part of the dogs behaviour. i.e. dog rushes the gate. How do we reduce the incidence of poor behaviour. By managing the consequences introducing a replacement behaviour, we can begin to produce better behaviours. Consequences can maintain a behaviour through the following: a) escaping something when the behaviour is shown-  dog cringes when handler says no, handler doesn't follow through,  b) dog gets a reward from the behaviour- dog jumps on hander when he sees them handler pats dog, dog is rewarded for the behaviour c)Something is provide a functional reward by the behaviour- dog has food handler moves to take food dog growls handler backs away d) something is avoided via the behaviour- handler wants to go home dog won't be caught , dog avoids going home and gets extra play time

The role of neurotransmitters such as dopamine on the dogs behaviour is relevant to training and teaching and how we do that successfully. Dopamine being released into the system is important for any training techniques to be successful, if we want positive behaviour then it is important to stimulate the release of dopamine into the body. Dogs who are not calm and enjoying what we are doing with them are going to have decreased ability to learn and grow positive skills. Similarly, a dog who has been left to self-reward for long periods of time may find reward triggers are easier earnt by reverting to the behaviours that previously triggered the release of dopamine in the body. So, learning for these dog needs to be planned out and worked through to achieve a total change in behaviours, four to five weeks to change the behaviours and to bring about positive changes to behaviour. Without though the positive input and the reward the dogs behaviour doesn't become naturalized because the reward base is not transferred,

The role of Serotonin in the body helps to keep the dog calm and healthy, promoting a good digestive system and healthy body and healing. If the dog is not being appropriately fed or if there are too many chemical stress triggers such as over vaccination poor quality food then the natural levels of serotonin can suffer and the natural mood stabilizer is no longer available to the dog. The benefit of ensuring health to benefit training is critical to the holistic view.

The question is and still remains is do we understand the behaviours we are seeing, do we understand cluster behaviours is every wagging tail seen as a happy dog or do we understand the tone of the wag. Behaviour is hugely affected by Dopamine, Serotonin and Noradrenaline and without patience and understanding the effect of each of these neurotransmitters on the body there is little change of successful and long lasting behavioral changes, in dogs or their handlers.

The immune system

How can  we support the immune system in the dog and support better behaviours, poor nutrition can have all the same effects on a dog as it would do to a human, tiredness allergy, depression, general lethargy, eating good healthy food can reduce the stress on the dog's body and increase their ability to be happier and healthier and reduce trigger stacking some of the choices we have included diets such as BARF- BARF is balanced raw feeding it stands for "Biologically Appropriate Raw Food " and is human consumption style raw diet that is based on 70 percent meat fish and bones and the remain 30 percent raw vegetable . This is said to mimic the natural food sources. Making sure that we carefully read the labels on any food we buy, always choosing to be careful about the food we buy so we can research the ingredients in any given label ensure that we purchase. Be aware of the ingredients in any commercial food especially dog food. Too often we overlook the labels of ingredients and we feel we are doing well by our dogs, but the ingredients list tells us exactly what is going into our bodies, dogs and people alike. Many dog owners are totally unaware of where their dog's food comes from and what the ingredients list actually mean and in some low cost brands or less ethical brands the ingredients may well be contrary to good nutrition. We should be aware of symptoms of allergies that can be the cause of poor food and nutrition some of the common symptoms of canine allergy include skin irritations, can be the dog constantly licking or scratching, wind, those horrible emissions expelled by dogs on poor diets, Hot spots where the skin one of the dog's organs breaks out in pussy, weepy sores that often require vet treatments. Asthma, just like people dogs can suffer from breathing difficulties when eating the wrong food, ear infection and inflammations, perhaps even leading to Aural hematomas due to scratching and the bursting of blood vessels, all of the above probably require vet treatments and can be expensive to treat after the fact, much easier to feed the dog better food and avoid needing treatments. For our shelter dog's it is important to put them on better quality food to compensate for the higher stress levels as quickly as possible. To ensure their bodies and their brains are ready for the future. Diet should be included in any behaviour modification plan and if not possible to change then at least the consideration of the role diet plays should be considered.

Medications can also impact on behaviour and it is important for any dog who is under a medical plan to have full disclosure of medications they may be on many medications can have serious side effects for example

Diphenhydramine, a frequently dispensed antihistamine, can be the cause of unwanted excitement and nervousness in canine patients.

Corticosteroid Which is a very commonly used to treat skin problems can make them less playful, less confident, more stressed, or nervous more fearful.
It is important that we consult with the dogs consulting Vet to ensure that any behaviour modification plan is not hindered by medication and to reduce the stress on an already overstressed dog.
Do we understand the part that confident handling plays in behaviour? Do we understand the debate of nature versus nurture? Do we understand the role that health plays in the role of behaviour-The overall general rule is if the dog is fed-all is well, and yet we are seeing more and more behaviour issues in animals that from an environmental point of view seem to be happy and well cared for. We know that stress plays a role in the digestive capabilities in dogs, and through the flight, fight or freeze theory we know that dogs who are in a constant state of stress are unlikely to be able to digest their food properly, resulting in more waste and less absorption of good nutrients throughout the body. Reduction in nutrients in the body reduce the ability of the body systems to work well. The nervous system being in a constant state of stress which in turn affects the digestive system, the digestive system without which nutrients cannot be properly processed on a cellular level. The health issues do not stop there though for a dog with poor health and poor nutrition the brain also becomes less open to growth and development. The brain needs its share of the bodies nutrients to grow and to allow for neural placicity. We know that through behaviour modification we can teach the dog to think differently and that by practicing positive techniques we can grow neural pathways and better manage behaviour. While the dog is unhealthy or unwell the dogs basic behaviours are compromised

Body language

Body language plays an important role in communicating in the canine world in socialisation and the importance of understanding that body language for the observer is crucial without an understanding of what we are watching we are unable to determine the mood and the motivation of the subject we are observing, practice, experience and intuition all take a place in the observation of any behaviour. There is much to understand though when watching dogs and understanding the play, today I watched a video of a dog licking another dog while holding its foot on its head. The second dog was younger, is a rescue in care and has been known to be reactive, she mouthed the other dog, who as stated was holding her down while standing erect and strong over the top of her and when she finally cracked and tried to bite him he chased her off and smacked her down. It was a simple exchange the dogs understood each other no blood was drawn and the bones was removed by a different dog. The little reactive dog has been under an intensive behaviour modification program to ensure that she is suitable for rehoming. So we were happy with the outcome, her behaviour modification plan has been to put her into a pack structure with a foster carer who supports our programs, attends puppy school and ensures that the dog is exposed to new environments in a safe manner. The dogs in the home are healthy well-balanced dogs who understand the rules, who play nicely and allow puppy license which is where an older dog allows a puppy to behave in a manner that an older dog would get disciplined for. The older dog gives grace to the puppy while it is learning new skills, the older dog may pin the puppy should it go too far or give other warnings but generally they are gentle with their disciplining of the younger puppy. And who will play in a self-handicapping way when needed. Self-handicapping is where the dog is playing with another dog who perhaps is smaller or less confident, in order to build the game and to increase the enjoyment for both dogs the stronger dog may offer a softer approach to the smaller dog. Including losing at tug of war and using less teeth when play biting. They will also back each other up without aggression if one dog is giving a warning the house sibling will walk through the middle and divert the foster dog. A safe environment but also one that without the puppy school and the outside excursions would not have been enough. But the building of resilience has seen the little dog be very successful.

For this little dog the puppy has been with us for most of her little life. But she is the product of several moves and different foster homes her brother who we separated from her at 8 – 10 weeks has been in one foster home and does not have the same issues, so we know there are no specific issues to cause her aggression, which originally was quite formidable and she would even take on adult dogs, something she did in a social class one day much to our horror this four month old puppy taking on a full grown bully type breed. Observation gave us poor behaviour in new situations no real trigger that we could see so the assumption had to be stress from many moves, we took her out of the round about, gave her an opportunity to develop resilience and then began to socialise her in new and strange environment with strange dogs.  If she had been an older dog with an unknown history we may have felt that she had suffered from social deprivation. Social deprivation and social regression are major issues for dogs and for people alike, We talk about healthy socialising and about ensuring our dogs are not strangers to noises and to other locations, including things like car rides the vets and activities we may over look though the importance that other dogs have on teaching our puppies to have a healthy outlook on life, studies show that Rhesus monkeys who were isolated for a major parts of their early lives didn't manage socially when placed with others of their species and also had reduced capacity to learn and to function, humans raised in isolation or in situations like the 13 American children recently rescued for abuse and isolation  also have limited development especially if they miss out on critical nurture at early stages of their lives. Puppies removed from their families before the right age, taken home and treated like mini humans are socially inept when introduced to others of their same species, they have no capacity to read body language of other dogs and are likely to respond in a way which will put them at risk when placed in a social environment. They may have not been socialised through that second crucial fear period and so when they again find themselves in company they are hesitant and cannot communicate well with others. We know that for this dog these are not the triggers,  For our little reactive dog Maddy, observation tells us that she became more stressed in new environments and when she was established in a steady home with healthy social dogs she was able to recover enough to find her forever home. The building of resilience has taken four weeks, lots of positives and allowing the influence and communication of other dogs. There is a lot to be said for the pack and the natural dog.

Where does the universe begin?

Anthropocentrism states that humans are the centre of the universe and that they are God made and everything is made for the comfort of Humans. Ecocentrism has the opposite view and states that each individual species is made as equal and denies the superiority of any individual species. Anthropomorphism is where humans attribute human characteristics to non-humans life forms, ie buying clothes for dogs so that they look like little people. Attributing human emotions. The danger for us when developing a behaviour modification plan is that we anthropomorphise and we decide that the dog will feel things in the same way that we do but this thinking gets us into trouble and brings about a lack of understanding of the canine, Although the dog has evolved to live with us and be part of our lives they still retain natural behaviours that see their methods of communicating differing from ours, We have an idea that dogs communicate in the same way as us however the dog reads body language they are visual dogs have evolved to read the right side of people's faces first as this is where human emotion is most strongly represented on a human's face. Some see this gaze as a sign of guilt where it is possibly just the dog watching us closely for a response.

we miss their subtle communications putting a human face n their behaviours. If we understand dog our dogs stress almost visually decreases, and behaviours can change very quickly. As Trainers we are not only looking at the behaviour but also the relationship between handler and dog, we are looking for a bond that is rich and encourages enjoyment and positive outcomes.  Training should be positive and develop this bond. Should an owner always be negative and always looking to punish the dog, there is no bond building and no way forwards for the dog. The dog needs to have positive reinforcement of good behaviours. Most dogs are human pleasers, they want their humans to be happy and they want to do what pleases their humans.  Our miscommunication confuses the dog and has his negative behaviours being reinforced rather than his positive behaviours. Most training of dogs needs to start with the owner. Teaching the owner to read body language, to understand what they want from their relationship with their dog and to understand the dog's relationship in their home and in their lives, is the first step of any form of training. As humans if we can communicate clearly with our dog a large part of the training issues will be resolved. Behaviour training should be a positive experience for both dog and handler, and humans and dogs are no different when it comes to being praised and encouraged, both perform better and learn faster when the dopamine is released into the system. Our responsibility to our canine friends and family is to an Ecocentrism approach rather than an Anthropomorphic view point.

Fear may be a factor in managing behaviour and may develop later in life as a result of a number of causes, such as: poor socialisation from puppy hood. The puppy may never have been exposed to any other dogs, environments and even noises as a puppy and then when exposure happens the dog perhaps doesn't have the emotional ability to process new things. A traumatic event such as a dog attack may also cause the dog/puppy to fear other dogs.. Rehoming- the dog may be subject to whole new environment without meaning too new handlers may not be able to provide the dog with the confidence it requires to make the move. The more moves the worse this can be.

Genetic Inheritance

Genetic inheritance can also be a factor in anxiety inherited from a mother who is predisposed to the stress or in a stressful situation. Harsh training methods-

Abuse- A dog who is exposed to harsh methods of training and perhaps hit or punished and not given balanced training may also become afraid.

Separation anxiety can become a major concern with dogs who have had multiple moves. Separation anxiety is the stress trigger for a dog left alone in any setting it may be at home, at Vets anywhere the dog is separated from its primary care giver. it can be very stressful for the dog and can include panting, vocalising, destructive behaviour, pacing, and many other symptoms.

Sensitivity to noises, sound and visual triggers may also cause fear such as thunderstorm phobias, the rumbling of thunder may cause the dog to salivate pant heavily and even in great duress escape and cause themselves harm, or to even end up in the pound, these types of fear triggers are hard to resolve without a lot of hard work and a safe environment for the dog so they can be protected in times of high stress.

Dogs experiencing fear are obvious fear where the dog is wary head dog licking lips tail between their legs showing deliberate body signals of nervousness, the dog would prefer to move away from the trigger given the choice, although given no choice the dog may display fight behaviours if flight is take away. Frustration is a second response to fear the dog may be uncertain of others in the environment and may be not be able to properly express the appropriate behaviours to the fear trigger, this may be caused by barriers such as fences or even lead, the dog is constantly confronted with the trigger but has limited capacity to resolve the issue. Dogs may display a variety of mixed signals they may hold hackles high tail elevated, pull on the lead, show no focus on the handler at all, may display some willingness to play then at the slightest miscommunication from either the handler or another dog the frustration releases, it's important to move the dog away and revisit the trigger after the dog is calm and focused on the handler. Also, it is important to match the dog with appropriate dogs so that no inadvertent challenges or poor language skills confuse the issue.

Fear aggression and reactive behaviour can be life threatening to the dog, A dog who has fear aggression and bites or attacks other dogs or handlers face the prospect of euthanasia. Euthanasia in its self is not a bad thing the gentle sleep offered by the euthanasia drug lets the dog drift into oblivion, but we who are left behind have the heartache of wondering what we could do differently, do we have enough information and is there something we missed. This is why our behaviour management plan is an essential tool, why understanding the dog, the handler and the environment is key to success why observation is so very important.

Applied behaviour is the observation, functional assessment and behaviour coaching of any individual handler and their dog to prevent poor behaviours and to train replacement behaviours through positive and rewards based training. The act of understanding the behaviour through the functional assessment and the ABC method to achieve positive outcomes.

The purpose behind a functional assessment is to determine the behaviour of the dog in any given circumstance, to determine the antecedent, the behaviour and the consequence without determining each of the above putting a behaviour plan into action is impossible. You need to be able to observe and watch and understand the relationship between owner and pet, this is what makes up the functional assessment.

It is important to remember the human cost of working with animals compassion fatigue is the definition given to people who are burn out as a result of too much impact from negative emotions as trainers we need to ensure that our methods support and work towards positive outcomes. Too many failures equal heartbreak and compassion fatigue it is important to be constantly moving forwards and achieving more. There are  five major perspectives in psychology:
- Biological: the nervous system hormones and genetic makeup, and how they affect behaviour
- Psychodynamic: How unconscious drives i.e sex and experiences affect our behaviour.
- Behavioral: the belief that behaviour is shaped by external environmental influences and that behaviour can be shaped
- Cognitive: that behaviour Is affected by your expectations and emotions
- Humanistic: everyone is good and we are all motivated to realise full potential.

Resilience

Resilience is an important part of achieving good outcomes the tools of emotional resilience are a sense of purpose, confidence, communication, flexibility, healthy relationships and humor. When we look at our relationships with handlers and their dogs we need to be coming from a healthy place, otherwise we are jaded and too easily discouraged, it is important to love what we do and to be able to share the passion with our clients and those we are training, if we want others to feel the excitement encouragement and a sense of hope that should be attached to our behaviour modification plan then we need to be enthusiastic and resilient enough to share it with passion and hope. The mindset is unique to every individual and is decided by 3 things, How a person sees themselves, how a person sees others, and how a person sees the world. If a person sees themselves as a failure this will impact on all the other parts of the mindset.

Honestly nothing is better than the realisation of the trigger and the way to resolve the behaviour. Seeing the bond build is the best outcome anyone could hope for. Emotional Intelligence is the understanding of who you are and where you are at, your personality the things that trigger you or encourage you and give you strength. The things you need to do for yourself to be healthy and whole and the best you can be.

The four components of emotional intelligence are Self-regulation- can you see what is happening and manage it? Social awareness- how you feel about others and how it affects you, self-management- can you control what you are feeling and adapt to what's happening around you, social skills- are you capable of good relationships and all that entails these are key skills to help us better communicate with the client to achieve those fantastic outcomes.

So we have achieved the Observation we understand the behaviour we can see the consequences, now we need to implement the change. There are so many ways we can assist with this, firstly we are ensuring that there are no health issues that the dogs Vet feels is causing the behavioural issues. If there were medicinal causes or issues with medication then our role would need to be completely different and be more focused on managing the behaviour rather than modifying the behaviour. Important to remember. Pushing a dog who has medical causes can add to their stress and amplify the behavioural issues.

Medical intervention can be one way of reducing stress or anxiety in the dog again only to be prescribed by a vet, however there are many Natural remedies that are safe for dogs. Natural remedies are often over looked because Veterinarians are not taught the practical applications of natural remedies and because the ease of using chemicals that work is far simpler than finding availability in areas of natural remedies. Essential oils and other products such as Bach flower Remedies these were developed in the 1930's by a bacteriologist and pathologist, Edward Bach Edward Bach a bacteriologist and pathologist, developed a range of flower remedies in the 1930's after being told he had very little time to live. In the 20 years that followed he developed a range of flower based remedies to help with balancing emotional and natural.
Complimentary responses

More and more we are seeing the use of complimentary approaches to animals and people's health and behaviour.  It is no longer a "one size fits all" approach and we are seeing an emergence of all types of ideas and solutions to what ails us. With the advent of internet and an ease of gaining knowledge on whatever subject you like the issue is actually having sense enough to not jump into every fad action but rather to research properly the methods and remedies that we feel we would like to implement into our lives, the real challenge is to ensure that we are gaining true knowledge. The other side of this is that the access to the internet is huge and any one can post anything sell anything and proclaim anything with no real foundation, leaving people disappointed and worse. The importance of studies such as randomised controlled trials help us to make informed choices. A randomised controlled trial is a trial where a series of individuals are treated with a medication, the trial includes both a placebo and the actual medication being tested. Neither the participants or the practitioners know which medication they are receiving / providing and the results are then translated at the end of the study.

For dogs struggling with ongoing stress essential oils may well be a support to the dog and their handler, various mixes work well on the nervous system giving relaxation and reducing the stress triggers, the added advantage is that some of these oils may well work on calming the handler as well. A test using lavender/ cedar-wood oil in the shelter has been encouraging and has seen a relaxed and calm attitude in the dogs. Other mixes may well support the immune system and release stress and give the handler a simple solution to calm their own stress levels as well. Many years ago I had a client in the vet clinic I was working in and the little dog was a mess we used a pheromone spray on the dogs bandanna and the calming was almost instantaneous what really made me pay attention was the effect on the owner. The owner became less agitated and this further relaxed the dog. One of the Vets I worked with used the Bach flower remedies as well on patients and again the impact on the owners was quite significant, their belief in the possible outcomes was almost a placebo effect to the owners. The owners had a concrete ability to do something to reduce the dogs stress, they began to reduce their own stress levels and the dogs stress levels went down as well. Amazing how often the reduction of stress in the handler miraculously reduces stress in the dog.
If we further use natural therapies we can look at natural physical therapies there are many massage therapies in different styles as well as acupuncture and hydrotherapy. Of course, as always when using these techniques to help as sore or injured dog it is important to get Veterinarian feedback first and to use a trained professional to carry out these techniques. However the use of canine massage therapy has great health benefits for any dog the theory of massage being that the muscles are relaxed and release pressure on nerves and body structure and the

massage therapy allows the blood flow to increase, reduces tension and the body is able to more efficiently able to send nutrient throughout the body, the release of tension also allows for the body to more easily send neurotransmitters throughout the body allowing nerves to better communicate with the brain, Some of the benefits of CMT include: emotional recovery, endorphin release, increased flexibility, pain reduction and stress release. All these things lead to an improved overall well-being.

The two expected responses to massage therapy are Relaxation Response, the animal is more relaxed the nerve centres are released and the animals blood flow increases to areas affected by stress and the endorphins released to the brain begin to respond positively and to increase the dogs feeling of wellbeing. Reduction of stress allows the brain to respond rather than to react and the dog becomes calmer and more relaxed. An involuntary but predictable response of the nervous system. Mechanical Response: the dog becomes calmer and pain and injury are relaxed through the massage allowing better healing to localised areas increase blood flows helps with healing and the release of stress allows the body's immune system to kick in and perform better which in turn allows for better healing better natural pain relief from the body. Physical effects occur in the body as a response to pressure applied to tissue.

T Touch is another method of massage and touch activities including wraps and other touch style methods based on the theory that posture can affect the emotional and physical wellbeing of a dog. Use of TTouch methods is said to be useful for all sorts of behaviour and health concerns from car sickness, aggression, leash-pulling, excessive barking and chewing, excitability and fear responses through to ageing.

Whatever the method massage certainly has positive effects on the bond between dog and handler. While an inexperienced handler should not be giving manipulation style massage gentle contact between handler and dog is a great way to encourage the bond, calm both the dog and the owner and encourage mental wellbeing for both.

The behaviour plan

Having wandered through behaviour, the causes and the consequences, we've managed to observe the behaviour and the handler. Now the time has come to set the behaviour modification plan. The plan should include any goals that the handler themselves want to achieve, it should include a detailed and carefully thought out action sheet with achievable goals and should give the handler the opportunity to achieve small goals along the way so that success can be measured. Part one of the plan what we want to achieve, what are the goals for some people this will be simple obedience recall and social behaviour, for the shelter the behaviour plan should include these things  also but should also look to build resilience and confidence in the dog to ensure that if they get moved multiple times before they find their forever home that they are able to maintain positive and stress free behaviours, one of the methods we can use for this is structure and asking for replacement behaviours for activities that would cause over excitement or aggression in the shelter. Simple activities like sitting before the gate to the kennel is opened. teaching stationing, crate training, all activities that can be transferred into their foster homes and their forever home, key behaviours that receive positive rewards and encourages the neural pathways into accepting the new behaviours permanently building towards extinction behaviours of the poor behaviours.

Consequences need to be measurable and achievable. While food is a great reward it is not always easily reached to support the reward of positive behaviours. Encouraging handler to focus on positives and give rewards that are verbal or physical- the pat for example that encourage better behaviours.

Encouraging handlers to record by video and by journal what is happening on a daily basis so they can go back through the behaviours or come back to you with questions, the visual footage helps both the handler and the trainer to see the Antecedent and behaviour to help to improve the consequences.

For the shelter dogs, it is important that any carer of the dog understands the behaviour modification plan and has the skill set required to support the behaviour modification plan.

Overall Managing Canine Behaviour Modification can be difficult as you are not only dealing with the dog but you are also dealing with handlers and every changing environment, being calm and confident able to articulate the plan and the reasons what the plan is needed is an important aspect of being successful, understanding who the dog is and where it came from, evolution body function stress responses and even nutrition are the first step in setting the dog and handler up for success. Understanding learning theory and training methods is what gives us the capacity to support the dog and the handler into a successful partnership that for us at the shelter see the dog successful in its new home, and for clients that sees long lasting relationships with great bonds, and handlers who are willing to do anything for their pet.

References

The scientist "origin of Domestic Dogs"
Wikipedia    "Evolution of the Wolf"
The Atlantic   " A new Origin Story for Dgs"

BBC Earth- " A Soviet Scientist"
National Geographic- "Taming the wild fox"
Professor Stanley Coren- The intelligence of Dogs
Howard Gardiner- Multiple intelligences
Richard Corey – Telegraph UK
John W Pilley – findings
Nicolas Wade-New York Times


What Do Dogs See in Mirrors?
They're not looking at themselves, but mirrors aren't meaningless to dogs
By Julie Hecht on August 31, 2017

What Does a Dog See in a Mirror?

By Melissa Dahl

WEIRD & WILD
What Do Animals See in the Mirror?
Asian elephants, magpies, and great apes are among the species that can self-recognize.
BY LIZ LANGLEY, FOR NATIONAL GEOGRAPHIC

Norepinephrine - Wikipedia
https://en.wikipedia.org/wiki/Norepinephrine


Serotonin: What You Need to Know


Medically reviewed by Debra Rose Wilson, PhD, MSN, RN, IBCLC, AHN-BC, CHT on May 18, 2017 — Written by Annamarya Scaccia


Serotonin - Wikipedia
https://en.wikipedia.org/wiki/Serotonin

Dopamine - Wikipedia
https://en.wikipedia.org/wiki/Dopamine


[Dopamine: not just a neurotransmitter]. - NCBI
https://www.ncbi.nlm.nih.gov/pubmed/16106242


Dopamine | Psychology Today Australia
https://www.psychologytoday.com/au/basics/dopamine


**Yorkshire Terriers | Temperament & Personality - PetWave**
https://www.petwave.com/Dogs/Breeds/Yorkshire-Terrier/Personality.aspx


Yorkshire Terrier Temperament: What's Good About 'Em, What's Bad About 'Em

Yorkshire Terrier Temperament, Personality, Behavior, Traits, and Characteristics, by Michele Welton. Copyright © 2000-2018


Yorkshire Terrier

From Wikipedia, the free encyclopedia

B.F. Skinner | Operant Conditioning | Simply Psychology
https://www.simplypsychology.org/operant-conditioning.html

Operant conditioning - Wikipedia
https://en.wikipedia.org/wiki/Operant_conditioning



UConn Researcher: Dopamine Not About Pleasure (Anymore)
November 30, 2012 - Christine Buckley - College of Liberal Arts and Sciences

OUT OF THE FOG
LEARNED HELPLESSNESS

ABC: Antecedent, Behavior, Consequence
This educational strategy seeks to mold student behavior
Jerry Webster
Updated May 07, 2018


Marc Bekoff Ph.D.
Animal Emotions
Dog Training's Dirty Little Secret: Anyone Can Legally Do It
Dog training is an unregulated industry although dogs need to be licensed
Posted Jan 19, 2017
"OCCUPATIONAL LICENSURE FOR PET DOG TRAINERS: DOGS ARE NOT THE ONLY ONES WHO SHOULD BE LICENSED," Elizabeth Foubert

is complementary and Alternative Medication right for your dog?
By Lisa M. Gillespie, April 2009

Complementary and Alternative Medicine for Pets
By Julie Edgar

The Use of Complementary and alternative therapies in dogs and cats with cancer
Lana SE, et al. J Am Anim Hosp Assoc

Pat Princi-Jones April 2018
Aromatherapy advocate, expert and educator @ Heritage Brands Pty Ltd

Pet Aromatherapy And Essential Oils: What You Need To Know
By Dr. Richard Palmquist, Contributor
Chief of Integrative Health Services at Centinela Animal Hospital, Inglewood California
Why Essential Oils And Pets Do Not Mix
Posted on 28 February 2018 by Dr Kevin Foster

5 Benefits Of Touch Therapy For Your Dog
by
Claire Hughes

How to Use Touch Therapy to Heal Your Dog
energy practitioner and animal communicator Cindy Brody

Overend Orthopaedic Animal Therapy and Rehab
EMMA OVEREND

Google search
Massaging your Senior Dog to Better Health by Ann-Marie Fleming

https://www.northnowravet.com.au/pet-joints/
BAD JOINTS